Little Waves

Patricia Gotuaco

Little Waves

Patricia Gotuaco
An Autobiography

EDITOR

Christina Gotuaco
Eldest grandchild

ILLUSTRATOR

Cassandra "Casey" Gotuaco
Youngest grandchild

– Otuaco –
2016

First Edition: 2016
ISBN 978-1-329-87949-2

Otuaco | San Francisco, CA
www.otuaco.org

To my grandmother who made it her life's project to support her husband's projects. Cheers to the years, the fun, and the recounting of an equally unique and endearing story.

LITTLE WAVES

*Illustration

BIRTH

I'm named after my father. I could have also been named Georgia after George Washington, you know, George Washington's Day. I'm glad I was named Patricia.

I had a nickname at home; they called me 'Dida' because I kept trying to pronounce my name, Patricia, and I kept saying Dida. That's why everyone calls me Di, except for Glo. She calls me Pat.

— ∞ —

I was born in 1936 on February 22, about 6 p.m. at Children's Hospital in San Francisco on California. My mom was twenty-five. She's 1911 and my dad was 1908 which makes him twenty-eight.

Glo was born in March 1940 then next April was Syl. The two of them were really close in age. They were one year apart.

— ∞ —

We were in Chinatown, San Francisco. My earliest memory was I was in a crib, and I was chewing the paint. Later I read somewhere that you're not supposed to.

SIBLINGS & EARLY CHILDHOOD

Auntie Glo was born when we were in Oakland. Stanley and Eva Moy, family friends, were asked to take care of me. He worked for Pan Am. They were good friends of my parents. I don't know how long I stayed with them; it was a short time, probably a week or so. No one said "Your mom's giving birth." They just said, "You're going to go stay with them." I was four.

I remember Auntie Eva was trying to comb my hair and she didn't know how to do it – she said because she didn't have any girls. I had ringlets.

They had a boy who was one year younger than me, Michael. We had tipped over their goldfish bowl and the fish fell on the floor.

It was warm there in Oakland. All I remember was the fish and the hair.

— ∞ —

We lived in San Francisco in an apartment building. My grandma owned it. But part of the time we were living in Oakland too, up to the time when I was four before my sister Glo was born.

Then about the time I was five we moved to Malaysia. It was called Malaya at that time. And my dad was working there until the Second World War started, and that's where my sister Syl was born.

Auntie Syl was born at home because I remember we had people come into the house – my aunts. One of them said, "You see the bird there? That's a stork!"

I was out in the garden and I remember saying, "I don't see any bird!"

— ∞ —

When Auntie Syl was eight months old World War II started.

We were in Malaya and it was war time. She was left behind when my mother – the three of us – went on a refugee ship back to the United States, because you could only take two children. No men and two children.

Syl was only ten months old. They gave her to the doctor who brought her into the world.

After seeing us off to the refugee ship, my father went back to look for them to pick her up and somehow get out of Malaysia and out of the way of the Japanese, but he couldn't find them because they had fled to the mountains.

So my father left. He went through China and into Europe and then to the U.S.

— ∞ —

We traveled at night from Kuala Lumpur to Singapore by car. When we stopped off somewhere at Singapore, I was trying to be friendly to somebody's dog. It was a police dog. It barked at me, and I got scared.

And then from Singapore we went by refugee ship to Australia as a stopping point, and then to New Orleans, because there was a lot of fighting in the Pacific so we couldn't go through it – submarines and aircraft strikes.

So we went through the Panama Canal.

The refugee ship was supposed to be only women and children on board but two men snuck on.

WARTIME & HOME LIFE IN THE U.S.

In those days you never locked your front door. You didn't need keys either. I lived on Clay Street between Powell and Mason.

My dad had a steady job with the Chinese Foreign Service. And then my mother had a job during the war. She went to work with a navigation line, it was some war effort, for a couple of years.

She worked the night shift. He went to work during the day and when he came back she had made dinner.

— ∞ —

My father liked to try out different restaurants and different ethnic foods, so we would go out to eat.

Stanley and Eva lived in Menlo Park. There were two eating places down in that area that my folks used to bring us to, buffets. One was called Ricky's. I bet you it's still there, or something like it. There was another one that was also pretty famous.

That's about the time when my sister fell out of the car and I didn't say anything.

We were coming back from a football game or something. My sister and I were in the back seat. The car did a turn onto a lane before the highway and the door wasn't shut properly so it swung open and as it did, she fell out. I have visions of her falling out. I was so shocked I didn't say anything.

My folks never scolded me for that. My dad looked in the rear view mirror before getting on the highway and saw a little thing running to catch up with the car – it was her.

They tied a handkerchief around her knee because she was bleeding a little bit and that was it.

So that was a funny incident. Glo keeps saying, "I bet you really wanted me to disappear." I should've been disciplined for it, but I remember it because I wasn't.

— ∞ —

When I was eight or nine and we went to visit Stanley and Eva. They weren't home and Auntie Glo stuck her hand in a bush and got stung by a bee.

— ∞ —

In those days they had news documentaries since they didn't have any TV. You'd go to the movies once a week and they'd have news documentaries about what was going on in the war.

During the war they'd have air raid sirens and you were supposed to turn off the lights in the house and then pull the shades down.

There were certain things in school that we had to do: We had to save metal and save aluminum. On chewing gum, we had to save the wrappers. This was for the war effort. You'd ball it up and bring it in to school.

Everyone in my class wore dog tags with their name and address just in case there was a war and a bombing. My parents never gave one to me or signed me up for one. I don't know why. I wanted one.

— ∞ —

There were food rations. Every how often we'd get these booklets with red points and blue points. Actually they were cardboard circles. Red points were for the meat; you could bring these to the grocery store to buy your meat, but you had to show these coupons. You could only buy so much.

I remember my uncle giving us his red coupons so we could have more meat. The blue points were for milk. I think it was for eggs too but I'm not sure about that.

So we couldn't hoard.

— ∞ —

I remember when the atomic bomb occurred, we just saw it over and over and over. And my father said it was very important. It was like a mushroom cloud. He was fascinated by it.

I was maybe seven or eight. The war was over when I was nine.

GRADE SCHOOL

My father always made us feel a little different. He wasn't typical Cantonese; he came from northern China. We didn't go to the local school. We went to a school that had a mixture of foreign kids. It was part of a program that San Francisco State had.

I didn't know until later that they had different ethnic groups: people who were Mexican, Scandinavian, Ecuadorian, Italian – a sprinkling of this and that. It wasn't just all Chinese. In fact, all the Chinese were people in the school who we knew.
We carpooled.

They were all the same class of people; there wasn't any big divide.

— ∞ —

At the beginning of the semester they'd fit you ergonomically. They'd put you in a chair and see if your feet touched the floor. If they didn't, they'd fit you with another chair.

— ∞ —

We were the guinea pigs of the teachers. They would practice new stuff on us. For example, there was a book of poems, an anthology, and they would ask us which poems we preferred for inclusion in the book.

We had to do a project to show which way the wind was blowing. It's like a sock. You post it on something and tell which way the wind was blowing.

Another was making a farm. We had to make a silo out of oatmeal cans, a silo for wheat grain. You made a floorplan of it with the cans. There was a farmhouse, and a silo, and a fence, and some plastic animals. That's when we were really small.

Making plants out of avocado seeds: You get an avocado seed and poke toothpicks in it, then put it over a glass of water and there's roots that grow out of it. We did many of them, but we never did anything with the seed after that except dump them away at the end of the school year.

But we did not have any chemistry type of projects.

— ∞ —

We didn't have any homework at all. We were so happy. We kind of just gloated over the other kids. We had no homework, and our school ended early. Everyone else's school ended at 4 p.m. and ours ended at 3 p.m.

We had individualized instruction. You did a workbook, and when you finished the workbook, you moved on to the next one so you could have different people at different levels.

— ∞ —

In first grade, they had a series called Fun with Dick and Jane – the readers. And you would sit in small groups with kids your level and you'd just keep on going. They had projects for you and you'd keep going on an individual level. If you needed help you could ask the teacher.

They always had instructions for the teachers in the workbooks, on the side in small print. You could read what it was.

That was especially fun for first grade because you weren't supposed to be able to read. On the side it would say, 'Ask the pupils to do this…'

— ∞ —

There would be projects everyone did together like science when you all got together and did a science project.

But reading and math, they just gave you workbooks and told you to do the workbooks.

They'd give you these certificates to show you you'd passed grade lower fourth then go to higher fourth, then lower fifth and higher fifth. And that's pretty much how I got through school. I skipped two levels that way.

It's sort of hard when you're skipping levels because you lose some of your friends. If you got bumped up, you'd go to the homeroom with the grade seven teacher, for example, with a whole bunch of other kids.

And they'd always put you in the front because I'm short.

— ∞ —

The whole day you were staying in the same room but the different teachers would come in.

The average of the class would have a lesson for the day, but if you were ahead you would just work on your stuff, and if you had a question you would raise your hand and she would come. That seemed to work out pretty well. Maybe about four or five of us were ahead. It's hard to say.

If you get too far ahead then they bump you up to the next grade, then you start with everyone being average again. But it makes you very flexible. At the end of the semester, if they wanted to bump you up they'd bump you up then. Then you'd gather up all your books and stuff, pencils and erasers, and go to the next room.

I only had problems with math. I could do the regular math but for the problem solving, I was very average.

— ∞ —

One time I had to write up a paper about carburetors. You'd have to go wherever you wanted to go and look up information on it. Of course in those days they didn't have any TV or computers.

The library was across the street from my grandmother's place. It was called North Beach Branch Library. It was on Powell Street between Washington and Jackson, and it's still there. I must have gone to the North Beach Branch Library and looked it up in the Encyclopedia Britannica or something like that.

I don't remember if I chose it or if it was assigned to me but I remember being so excited. It was something I didn't know anything about, and now I did. I just remember thinking, 'This is what it's all about!'

— ∞ —

In school, when you became seventh or eighth grade you also became a school monitor. You were given notices to distribute with a bunch of papers to the different classes, that type of stuff. You supervised the lunch room. You and other people would set up the tables and the napkins and other stuff, and see to it that the kids eat properly.

There were hot lunches and cold lunches. For hot lunches, you paid $1.25 for the week. The cold lunches were you-bring-your-own. You had a choice, either you could bring your own or eat there in school. We always had hot lunch.

There was a macaroni and cheese that I didn't like, that was the one I remember; some sort of stew and some sort of beans; and milk in cartons.

— ∞ —

I got a decathlon medal one time. I used to run very fast. They had a big area and you'd just run back and forth. They always had people testing you out about how high you could jump from a standing position and stuff like that.

They had softball. I hated being shortstop because you're so close to being hit. I preferred being a baseman.

— ∞ —

They had wonderful murals on the wall, just like Coit Tower, inside near the principal's office – scenes of people working, murals of farmers and engineers and doctors and stuff like that.

I was very impressed with Coit Tower; that was a field trip of ours. We must've went on a bus and a streetcar.

We went to 4th and Townsend as one of the field trips, to the train station. We went inside the train.

I think we should've gone to the Mint because it was so close by but I can't remember that.

We went to some park for a May Day festival.

— ∞ —

The thing I was most proud of was when I was eleven, and when my sister got sick, my mother didn't have to bring us to school. We usually took the street car, and I took it by myself. I was really proud of that.

My school was at Laguna and Market. It became UCSF something or other up there, but they knocked it down just recently.

— ∞ —

Six years I was there. I started in grade one and graduated from eighth grade. There were eight grades, with two levels in each grade and maybe about twenty or twenty-five kids in each.

It's funny, even now when you mention the name of someone, I could tell you the first or last name of them. And you sort of wonder, what happened to these people? Because a lot of them I only had them for one or two years because I kept on moving.

I have one eighth grade teacher, she's still alive. I think one day I'd like to look her up. I still send her Christmas cards.

GROWING UP IN SAN FRANCISCO

There's a park there at the top of Nob Hill with a sandbox and it was just about a block or two away from where we lived on Clay Street, and we would go to that sandbox. It was a big circle, and we would make mud pies, my sister and I.

One day this white lady came by, this American lady, and she asked, "What are you doing?" And we said, "Making mud pies." And she said, "Are they for sale?" And we said, "Yes for ten cents."

And she gave us ten cents.

— ∞ —

There was another thing on Powell Street where the cable car turns up Jackson Street. This was during the war.

This one sailor was standing at the end of the cable car, the cable car jerked, and he fell over the end. He landed on the ground with his oranges, and he ran back and got back on the car because the cable car man saw him and slowed down. He was able to catch up with the cable car when it rounded the corner.

My sister and I were outside playing hopscotch. That was a big deal back then in those days, with your keychains as your markers.

And jump rope.

— ∞ —

I think we were at 1178 Clay Street. The rent there was $60 a month. There were two flats; we lived in the lower one.

It had a Spanish design, two bedrooms and a bath. The toilet was separate by itself. The bathroom had a bathtub and a shower, and it had black and pink tiles very typical of that time. That was back in 1942-1948.

It had those tiled steps and once in a while going up the stairs it had that Spanish tile. It had a two car garage; we had one. I don't know if the people upstairs were owners or renters. The kitchen had a wrought iron stove.

It had a dining room and a dinette. The dining room was more formal, where we never ate, and the dinette was where we always ate.

— ∞ —

My mom cooked, it was Chinese mostly – some fried veggies, meat, pork shoulder, with soy sauce.

We never had snack food in the house. There was nothing at all. And we never had sweets or desserts. I don't know why we didn't.

— ∞ —

I didn't have much appetite as a child. There was one dish I really liked – bok choy with bean curd. There was one restaurant in Chinatown that had it, Nam Yuen, that I liked the best, and I would always order that one dish.

There was a time when I liked licorice sticks and pickles, and a time when I liked char siu right when it came out from being roasted. They would take it out and hook it up in the store windows and there were parts that would be burned, with a lot of fat to it, and if we were in Chinatown buying food and they happened to come out with that, we'd get it.

When I was a little girl I liked to eat rice with butter and soy sauce.

— ∞ —

I took piano lessons. We rented a piano and put it in the dining room. I think they must've got it in through the window. I came home from school one day and there it was.

My parents picked at it but didn't really play.

I took piano lessons when I was nine and that was sort of late. Other people started about six or seven. We went to the teacher's house. She lived on Jackson Street, so we walked over three blocks. She was a Caucasian woman, and if you played well she gave you stickers of flowers on your book.

— ∞ —

My grandma lived about three blocks away, my mom's mom. We ate a lot with her.

My grandma owned this house on Powell Street where she lived – 1122 Powell – and there were six apartments. She had two, and then her mother-in-law had one, and then my aunts shared one, and then my Auntie E was in the other one. So when we made dinner they'd all come down to eat it.

She had apartments 1 and 2 but they broke down the wall and it was one big apartment.

When my father went to Manila we moved into one of the apartments (number 5). They had been renting it out beforehand.

— ∞ —

When we were living on Clay Street, there were a group of friends of ours all about the same age, and we would play kick the can. The fun part about it was it was during night time.

You kick the can and everyone goes and hides, and the one who's 'it' gets the can and makes it upright, and then goes to look for the people who are missing. If he tags anyone, they're frozen. In the meantime, if you're one of the ones he's searching for and you go and kick the can again it frees everyone who was frozen.

It's a wonder my parents would let me go play on the street at night.

There were about five or six people. This was on Clay Street. There are some houses that have entryways so you'd hide behind there, behind a post or something like that. And it's supposed to be dark.

— ∞ —

The other thing we did was skate. We roller-skated down steep hills. Mason Street down the back is pretty steep. These were the old-time skates – four wheels and a key. Once you skated enough you got to be pretty good at it.

Mason Street between Clay and Washington is steep, so that was challenging. But Clay Street where the house was, was flat. That's where we learned how to skate.

We liked our skates so much that my father had a friend who brought some skates over to Manila. We skated where we stayed in Manila and the people underneath complained because it was so noisy. Those were good skates.

— ∞ —

I wore mostly blouses and skirts. My mom sewed outfits. She would make some of the skirts. The blouses we would buy in the store.

For Easter or something like that, she'd make outfits; matching.

We never wore pants much in those days. They didn't have jeans and stuff in those days.

— ∞ —

Mom used to wash the clothes and she would hang them on a line outside the back with clothespins, between our house and another structure. There were no washing machines. She used one of those washing boards.

All I remember was going to sleep and you could hear this scrub, scrub, scrub, at night time.

— ∞ —

There was a year there when Father was in Manila and we moved from Clay Street to my grandma's place. Mom took care of us for the year. That was a really great year. I was eleven and my father wasn't around to tell us what not to do.

We went down to where the 49ers used to play, near Golden Gate Park – Kezar Stadium – and rented bikes. And my mom showed my sister Gloria how to pedal (she was about six years old) but Mom forgot to tell her how to brake and how to turn, so she ran into a wall.

— ∞ —

That was the year I was able to go on the streetcar to go to school a few times so Mom didn't have to drive. And it was every time my sister got sick. I really didn't mind if she got sick; that was fun. I guess it was just a few times.

You felt so grown up because you had to go all the way down Powell Street from Washington and Jackson. You'd go all the way down to Market and then transfer to the Market Street car and get off at Laguna. I think it was five cents.

Afterwards when I came back and went to college, they had these transfers that you'd punch.

READING

I remember wanting to read so badly. We were driving to Chinatown one day and I said, "What does that say, and what does that say…" and Mom said, "That says Coca-Cola."

I liked to read everything. I don't know why I picked up on that Coca-Cola sign; maybe because it was red. She was very good about that. She was very supportive.

— ∞ —

She never said much. She was very quiet. But they had this series of girls' books and she'd buy them for me, the Maida series. I read almost all of them: Maida's Little Shop, Maida's Little Houseboat, Maida's Little Island, Maida's Little Zoo.

It's about a girl who was an orphan and she had a bunch of friends and they went on adventures together. That was one of my favorite books. What my mom did, she never said anything, but she knew I liked them and she bought the books for me.

The other one I didn't like so much was Honeybunch. It was sort of like Nancy Drew but for younger people.

— ∞ —

My father bought books for me because he didn't want me to cross the street to go to the library because he was afraid I'd get run over. So he bought Tom Sawyer. He tried to buy classics. Story of Mankind.

My Friend Flicka. He didn't buy that one but that was one of my favorites. That was at the library.

It was really funny: I had a thing about horses about that time, and we would go to the department store, the Emporium on Market Street, and my mom would leave me at the book department. And I'd get this book about horses and I'd read it and she'd leave me.

And then we'd come back and I'd pick the book back up again. She could always leave me there and know that I wouldn't be wandering around. It was about how to ride horses.

And I never rode a horse. Went to Baguio once and rode a pony.

Black Beauty was another one. This was when I was about eleven or ten.

The other one was Little House on the Prairie. At that time I didn't appreciate it as much as I would have later on, since it's really historical.

There was another book series of horses, The Black Stallion. I read maybe about four or five of them.

PETS

I had a bird that died or disappeared when I was four and living in Oakland.

I had a turtle that got stepped on.

The time when my sister was born we had a pet in a cage, and then we didn't have a pet and a cage. I don't know what happened to it.

My father had an aquarium with some fish. He went out to Geary Boulevard; there's a pet shop. He got some guppies. They swam into a little temple and one got stuck there.

— ∞ —

The turtle was when we were at Powell Street.

We had gotten it from Fisherman's Wharf at a stand. You could buy these turtles for fifty cents and they came in a box, and you could send them to anywhere in the United States.

One of those rectangular pots for plants was like a big swimming pool for the turtle so we had it there.

And then someone stepped on it by mistake because it had crawled under some newspapers. We had taken it out because we were playing with it, but I was going to put it back.

It was a playmate friend of ours. She was one of the Chinese who was going to the same school we were.

INVENTIONS

The first big deal was the ball pen in 1948. I was ten or eleven. It was the year that daddy was gone.

It was when I was in eighth grade. It was five dollars, and it was big. They didn't have the plastic ones. It was metal.

Before that, we were using pen and ink. You would have your pen and fill it up with ink. There's an ink bottle – Waterman was a brand – you put your pen inside the ink bottle and there was a little lever you push up and down and the ink goes in.

My mom gave it to me as a gift for Christmas. It was silver colored. It was bulky. It felt big. Five dollars was expensive in those days.

When we were in seventh or eighth grade practicing script was when we started using pens instead of pencils. They didn't want to give them to you younger than that because you would get ink all over the place. The desks had a hole where you could put the ink bottle.

I don't remember bringing stuff home from school. I think I just left it there.

— ∞ —

When we went to Bangkok in 1950 they did not have scotch tape; they used rubber bands.

When you buy something in the store and they wrap it with newspaper, they would use rubber bands to wrap it around the box. I thought that was interesting. Tape always seemed to be around, here.

— ∞ —

The first TV I saw was in 1952. It's when I came over to the States from Bangkok. There wasn't anything over there at the time. It was at grandma's house.

We didn't see colored TV until we moved into Galaxy. We moved into Galaxy in 1962.

— ∞ —

I saw my first washer and dryer when I stayed over at my cousin Janet's (her mom is my mom's sister, my mom is the oldest girl).

My mom got married in her twenties and Auntie Fran, Janet's mom, got married late. She actually didn't want her to get married because no one would take care of my grandma, but eventually she defied tradition and got married.

Janet's mom was so excited because she said, "Listen, it buzzes so you can tell when it's finished!" – the dryer. That's when they first moved into Diamond Heights in the 1960s. We didn't use them when I was growing up, but they were around a little earlier than that.

— ∞ —

On TV they had a show my grandmother watched. She didn't speak English, by choice, but she watched this show called Chef Cardini. He comes on with these two knives and sharpens the knives. And that's the only English she learned.

She actually was from here. Everyone here was from my mom's side. All the ones in China I never met since the Communists closed down travel between China and the U.S. in 1948.

So all of that part of my dad's family we never met until we went into China in 1990 or 1991.

WORLD EVENTS

I remember the atomic bomb because they kept showing pictures. There was a movie theater that always showed news and documentaries, and my father would always drag me along.

Auntie Glo was too young, she was only five. My mom didn't go – I think she was at work or something.

When the war ended, we were in San Francisco and on the front page of the newspaper the font was so big. The headlines were half a page, something about 'War's End' or 'End of War.'

Right after the war, they had a cartoon drawing, Kilroy Was Here. It was basically a guy with a big nose. GI soldiers would go to different parts of Europe and just put a logo there.

— ∞ —

The other big thing I remember was Mahatma Gandhi when he got killed. He got assassinated. There was no TV at that time so I guess it was in the papers or on the radio.

— ∞ —

And I remember the beginnings of the United Nations.

It was held in San Francisco and all these Chinese people would come to the house speaking something we don't understand (it was Mandarin). They would have all these meetings because it was the Chinese delegation, because my father was working with the Chinese consulate.

— ∞ —

When I was going to school in Bangkok, high school, King George died. King George is the father of Queen Elizabeth.

The British people that worked in the school wore black because they were in mourning for King George, but I don't remember what year that was. That was in the early '50s.

PARENTS & FAMILY

My dad spoke Mandarin but he didn't speak Cantonese, and my mom spoke Cantonese and not Mandarin, so we grew up speaking English. That's why we were so much better in English and no good in Chinese.

But my father learned Cantonese before my mom learned Mandarin, so it was more Cantonese.

— ∞ —

When my father and mother were dating, my grandmother on my mom's side didn't like my father because he 'wasn't Chinese' since he didn't speak Cantonese.

And my grandmother from his side, when she found out my dad was dating someone in the U.S., wanted to know what color hair she had.

That's the reason why we don't speak Chinese that much.

— ∞ —

Daddy was quite an artist. When we were in Manila, he'd have a wine bottle and melt a candle into it, then melt another one of a different color into it and we'd have bottles with wax dripping down it.

Or he'd do Chinese painting onto a lampshade.

— ∞ —

I never knew my grandfathers, they were both gone before I was born. And my grandmother in China, I never met her. She lived to be 100. Or so they say.

My father was in China at that time. The family asked him to go back to celebrate her birthday. He was afraid to because they were the Communist side, and he was on the other side, the Nationalists. And if they captured him, I remember him saying, "The U.S. would never go to war with China over me." So he never went.

— ∞ —

So the only grandparent I knew was my mom's mom. She was very nice. She remembered what I liked. She would get me this type of coffee candy she knew I liked when I came to college.

She was nice to me because I was one of the early grandchildren, and then there was a period of time when there were no grandchildren. My mom married young and my Auntie Fran married older so Janet, who is my cousin, is the same age as Gigi.

She had osteoporosis so her bones were soft and she couldn't really sit up at the very end. But she was very interesting when she was younger. She used to sew a lot – very fine Chinese embroidery.

She used to drink whiskey. She had a slot machine in her bedroom; Uncle Tim fixed it up. But one day someone broke in and the story is she broke a bottle of whiskey over his head. But when the police came to investigate they took her slot machine since it was illegal or something.

She knew English, but she didn't want to use it.

She had bound feet and it was hard to find shoes for her because she was a size 3 or 4. I think they were bound here. She was the third girl in the family. Number 4 didn't have bound feet.

— ∞ —

During the 1906 earthquake, number 4, my auntie, was able to run – she ran and took the ferry to Oakland.

We called her 'fourth auntie.' She was really nice. She lived on Grant Avenue at one of these Heritage sites (now). Everyone goes to visit her and she knows what happened to everybody.

"I haven't seen my brother in a long time," you'd say, and she would say, "He's doing this." She was like a switchboard – she knew what was going on with everyone.

She was very colorful. I found her very fascinating.

She would talk in Chinese and Sally would respond to her in English. I thought that was so cool.

— ∞ —

Angkong's mom speaks the same kind of Chinese, so it got better when I got married because I used it more, but it's still pretty awful.

But I practiced with my mother-in-law and when we came to the U.S. to visit, I spoke with my fourth auntie in Chinese.

She would have a big party every year and you'd see everyone. Number 3 would be there and we'd see everyone – Paula, Janet.

HIGH SCHOOL & CORRESPONDENCE SCHOOL IN MANILA

After I graduated from grade school in the U.S., then I went to Manila for two years.

When we got to Manila, my parents had to start dressing up. We didn't like Manila so much because our parents were so busy with other things. It wasn't like before.

It's from when I was twelve to fourteen.

— ∞ —

I had two years of high school. The first year I went to a school that was all girls.

It was the first time I was in an all-girls school. I went to Mary Knoll. It was not only all girls, but it was a Catholic school.

Up until that time I never knew there was such a thing as the Catholic Church. I was so sheltered.

It's funny, the girls at the school, they were sort of possessive. So you're in the class and they want to be your friend. When one wants to be your friend, you could only be friends with one, you couldn't be friends with the other or they'd get mad about that.

I wasn't used to that type of social interaction at all.

— ∞ —

The first year I went to Mary Knoll, then the second year I went to the American school.

The reason why I didn't go to the American school was they said they don't let Asians in. They were mostly white. But apparently my father made a big stink about it, since we were American citizens.

I didn't want to leave Mary Knoll because my friends were there, but my father said, "You're going to the American school." And during that time you just do what they tell you to do. When there were these issues, we weren't parties in these discussions.

— ∞ —

My third year of high school we went to Bangkok and I had a correspondence course for two years.

I was too old to go to my sister's grade school. She went to a British school where she had to learn pounds, shillings and pence, and I ended up in a correspondence course instead.

This American International School, I was taking extra. I took a course in Latin just for the heck of it. That's where I saw this British woman wearing the black dress for King George, for many weeks.

It wasn't too far from the area where they just had this bomb blow up at a Buddhist shrine.

— ∞ —

Correspondence school was something else – they sent you books and tests, and then you fill them out, take the test, send it back, and then they correct the test and send it back to you with remarks and grades. The main program of it was based in Baltimore.

For grade school there was the Calvert system and then the next level of it, I think, was called American School. A lot of people have a problem when they had kids and traveled.

It was self-tutored. If you had a question, you couldn't ask anyone.

I was very good in geometry and that was at Mary Knoll because it was so nice and logical. In correspondence school, I got second year algebra but no one was there to help out. My father must have been very busy at the time, usually he helps.

I remember that algebra book – the first twenty pages were dog-eared. I was trying to figure out what everything was and what they wanted me to do, but I looked at it and I was getting more and more frustrated.

I had to send back the booklet after a few weeks and switched to trigonometry. It was so much better.

In correspondence I also had a geography course and biology.

— ∞ —

My father was too busy to teach me, and my mother, I never asked her. I just remember that course and French. I had first and second year French, and I had a teacher who wrote and was just fascinated with someone who was living in Thailand.

'What is it like there, what do you do in your spare time?' I remember she used to write. I don't remember her name.

But it took a long time to send things – to send them by airmail then get them back. You don't have any feedback and you don't have any competition going to a school like that for two years.

— ∞ —

So at the end of the two years I had to apply for the SAT test.

They had to arrange it with the American embassy and when I took the SAT, I was in a room all by myself. It was a little room with some windows and no one was there. Someone came in to check on you, say "Do this part," leave, and come back again.

It was a three hour test, I think, and it was the longest test I ever had.

AUNTIE GLO

Auntie Glo, when we all went to Taipei, my parents sent her to boarding school in high school. My father didn't believe in the Catholic Church and he thought it was really restrictive, but he thought this school would be good for discipline. It was like a military academy.

It was in Taichung. That's why her Mandarin is good, because there were many Mandarin-speaking Chinese girls in that boarding school. Some of them now, when we go to her place for picnics and stuff like that, some of them are from that school.

— ∞ —

She was always very active and lively and very into a lot of things. She had a permanent set of crutches because she was always breaking things.

One time someone came to deliver packages from Bangkok and she got on his motorcycle and drove around the block. She was trying to find the brakes and stopped so fast that she flew off and broke something, her knee or arm. She was supposed to be confirmed in a Confirmation ceremony and this happened right before that.

She was always giving my parents a headache. When she was small, she got the most spankings of all.

— ∞ —

She's a really good storyteller and lots of fun, ever since she was a little girl.

By the time she got here, she went to Dominican for college which was a Catholic school but she wasn't Catholic.

She knows more about Catholicism than I do. She went to the Catholic schools.

— ∞ —

Auntie Glo ended up eloping. She and Mom drew up guest lists and planned and planned, and she wanted the reception here and she wanted it there.

They didn't agree on the wedding plans and then eventually she decided to elope. It ended up being on the same date we got married, but six years later.

EARLY EMPLOYMENT

When I started college my parents gave me $500 and when I graduated I went back and gave them $500.

I put it in the bank; Auntie Fran was the banker. She worked at Bank of America and helped me open an account. She was vice manager.

There's a branch in Chinatown and that's where she was.

— ∞ —

My first paid job was during Christmas. They hire you temporarily down at the department stores. My aunt helped me and I was hired at Joseph Magnin's.

I was supposed to be in the department where they sell fancy clothes, and I was supposed to be the assistant of the person who works in this department. That was only for about two or three weeks.

One time I was asked to deliver something somebody had bought to a home, and it was after hours because I remember it was dark, somewhere down Powell Street. So I took the streetcar, and I got a tip for it from the person I gave it to.

No one told me to take a cab, so I took a street car and walked a few blocks, then took the streetcar back and walked a few blocks. I guess they figured it took so long, so they never sent me to deliver something again.

My aunt, Janet's mom, helped me find that job. She was really nice. That was my freshman year at Mills. I was sixteen.

— ∞ —

My other first jobs were in school, waitressing work. It was 80 cents an hour.

You would just go to student employment in school and ask them what they had available.

My girlfriend did telephone operator and one night she shut down the whole school. She pushed the wrong button and no one could call in and no one could call out. She came back to the room and she was like, "Do you know what I did?"

Other people worked in the library. I liked doing waitressing work because you got to choose your pick of food. The cooks were Chinese and they'd save chicken skin for you, you know.

They had the worst noodles. They said they were cooking them for white people.

— ∞ —

You'd sign up for the meals you want, and we had a good group of friends from that. You learn how to carry trays on your shoulder and how to serve from the left and pick up from the right.

If you were the head waitress you made 80 cents an hour, as opposed to 60 cents, and you told other people the stations they were supposed to work at. I had a contract for ten hours a week, which was the equivalent of ten meals a week. It was time efficient; you have to eat anyway, so they let you eat first.

At that time, it was sit-down and each hall ate at a certain time, and now they've changed it to everyone eats in the same hall and now it's just cafeteria and very informal. It used to be you would eat in your separate hall where you stayed.

I guess it was about 100 people and we were each given two tables so there were about five or six servers at a time. If there was a special occasion, they would have people sitting at a head table, some faculty or some visiting parents. Then you'd get the better servers to serve them.

I was one of those for two or three years out of the four years. What you do is assign tables and just take care of anything that needs to be taken care of.

On Wednesdays and Sundays you had to dress up for meals. And those were the days I liked to serve so I didn't have to dress up.

— ∞ —

And then they sing blessings. It's a doxology. 'Praise God from whom all blessings flow.'

It's a Christian school, not a Catholic.

— ∞ —

The money that I earned – they paid you by month – I used that for incidentals, Kleenex, bus rides, and stuff like that.

I worked all four years. I didn't tell my father for the first two years because I knew he wouldn't like it. You know sort of like, my daughter doing such lowly work.

The other paying jobs I had was when I was working already, teaching.

UNDERGRADUATE STUDIES

I knew I wanted to do something in sociology because I knew I didn't want to do math and science. I don't have the aptitude for math; science is okay I guess. Sociology was studying groups of people.

You don't declare when you're a freshman yet, until the end of your sophomore year. My freshman year I took an introduction to sociology and it fascinated me!

I remember they had these charts about if you were upper class you would be reading these kinds of magazines, if you were middle class, you'd be reading these magazines, you'd be driving this kind of car, and going to this kind of school.

Demography – it explained different classes of people and their characteristics. It's just like psychology is the study of the individual and sociology is the study of groups of people.

I had sociology and economics as a double major.

— ∞ —

I was real picky about the way I wanted to say things, and usually you have a few papers at a time, not just one to do. It all sort of piles up on you.

There was a time when I was sitting out in front of my professor's cubby. You had to drop off the paper by 8 am so I was there sitting on the floor in the hallway revising or proofreading it.

You would use carbon paper and if you made a mistake you had to have little strips of paper to cover it, and then type it over.

I was in a coat because I was in my pajamas. That's usually what happens with 8 o'clock classes – you have pajamas underneath your coat and you go to class like that.

That was one all-nighter. I had a few scattered throughout the four years.

— ∞ —

At Mills when I was there, there were about a dozen Asian girls at most. There were so few that you pretty much knew everybody. They were from Hong Kong and Hawaii, and one or two from Indonesia.

And then we had international students from Greece and Germany and Canada.

A lot of girls came from California, one from Texas, some from New York and Boston but most from very near – Monterey, La Jolla, and Oregon. We considered them local. Chicago. Just about everyone was very friendly.

In our particular hall, there was a Catholic bunch. Some of us would go to mass every day, especially during Lent. We'd go to mass as group and then come back for breakfast – a small group, maybe about three or four of us.

I just remember it was cold.

— ∞ —

We had fire drills every semester and there was one girl who would refuse to come out for the fire drills, and she'd have to go up in front of the judicial board court.

— ∞ —

Phones were expensive. There was no phone in the room, just one down the hall on each floor. They had a buzzer system in the rooms.

The office for the hall was downstairs and they'd receive the call, and then they'd buzz you to let you know you had an incoming phone call, and then you'd go to the middle of the hall and wait for the call.

I had very few calls.

— ∞ —

In our hall, a Chinese girl was next to me. When she was a freshman, she and another girl were from China.

Someone decided it would be a good thing to put them together, but they were like night and day. One liked to go out a lot and party and go on lots of dates, and the other was very sober and serious and liked to study. The party one, her side of the room was all undone and messy. The other side was occupied by this Jane, and it was very neat.

They only lasted a semester, actually less than a semester.

Jane, the serious one, was Chinese from Manila. Her mother had died. Her father had married somebody else but didn't tell her. And they had a baby and hadn't told her until she graduated. When she was heading back they told her she had a baby brother.

— ∞ —

There were two groups of people – ABCs here and Chinese from China.

So when you're a freshman, this was the dating scene: the social committees for your hall would arrange for parties with the different fraternities. They would also include some of the Asian boys – the American-born Chinese and the Chinese from China – so you had a chance to meet people you could date eventually.

They'd have little socials. We had some girls at our school who were very social. I wasn't as social. Usually you'd go as a little group.

They did it with Stanford and Cal and some other schools. They would contact the fraternities to see if they were interested in getting together for these socials. There was some dancing and then you get to meet them and you could go out on dates afterwards. I usually ended up playing tennis with them.

There was this one boy from Hong Kong and he was very interested in going out on a date with me, but I didn't really like him. I had to fulfill my tennis requirement; he played tennis and I played tennis.

He was a biology major and went to Cal, and his father was a famous eye doctor in Hong Kong; he's still over there. My father said (because I wrote to my parents every week) I wrote to him and said I went on a date with this guy and so on, and my father said if he was smart enough he would have gone to medical school instead of getting a biology degree, if he wanted to be a doctor.

But usually people do get their biology degree if they want to be a doctor.

And there was another fellow, a very serious fellow, Chinese from China, and he brought me to see La Bohéme. And he got me the record my senior year. I listened to that when I was studying, so I really got to know that. He played tennis too.

I really wasn't interested in them, but I was really interested in getting through my PE requirements. You had to record a certain amount of time.

They had that, and before you graduated you had to pass a swim test. There were three things you had to pass: You had to swim fifty yards, tread water for three minutes, and you had to float for a certain amount of time.

And what's funny is that the president of our class couldn't pass the swim test until the last day. Everyone was there around the pool on the last day cheering her on and she finally passed. She just had to pass, she was a nice a girl.

— ∞ —

One time, I was a sophomore and my friend was a freshman, and we were in a little section of our hall where a couple of us were Asian. One was from Hawaii. We got to be really good friends.

One was Vivian, and she said she was going to barbeque stuff. She took the top of a garbage can and put coals on it, and did it up in her bedroom. She's so responsible and proper, she was president of her class, and almost president of the student body.

It was down on our end of the hall and the smoke was coming out. There was too much smoke so she said, "Open the window!" So we opened the window. Downstairs there were a bunch of seniors in some sort of procession in their cap and gowns and we were hoping no one would see, and no one looked up.

That was crazy. I don't know why we did that. It was sort of barbeque pork or something like that, and it worked! She's such a straight person that you wouldn't think she would do stuff like that. She also did Phi Beta Kappa.

I'm sure she must have had some kind of prior experience. It wasn't even her room; it was our other friend Franny's room.

— ∞ —

The other thing we would do is we would collect alarm clocks from everyone down the hall and someone would come back from a date really late, and we'd set them up to ring at different times throughout the night and hide them in her room.

Another thing is short-sheeting. This is for people who go out on dates and come back really late and a bit tipsy. You would fold the sheet so that they could only get in half way.

We studied very hard too you know.

— ∞ —

We corresponded a lot, Angkong and I, in my college years.

Everyone had their own mailbox you had to sign up for at the post office. Mine had a glass window so you could see if there was mail. I went twice a day, just in case he wrote.

And my father wrote once a week.

When we went to Bangkok, I had all these piles of letters and things so I kept my stuff with Auntie Fran in a back room of hers on Powell Street, along with my little doll I had since I was a year old, with all my college notes and stuff like that. And then they sold the building after I got married and I don't know what they did with everything.

The only letter I really do have is this one, from my father.

I would give anything for those letters. You can't blame Auntie Fran because she probably wrote to my mom and asked her, "What do I do with this?" And she probably told her to throw it away.

I don't think there was any public storage in those days.

— ∞ —

You know, in the '50s, the idea was more or less to get married and have a family.

And basically that was how we were brought up.

Most of the people that graduated about my time were following the same pattern. But before marriage, you have a job, and then more or less later you find someone, and then you get married.

COURTSHIP

Between the two of us, our parents knew each other – nice family and nice family.

He's the youngest boy.

His mother liked having her sons meet nice Chinese girls, so they would have dancing parties thrown by an older relative in their house.

At that time I was thirteen or fourteen, and I remember going to a party and I had to go by myself because my sister was so much younger, she wouldn't fit in. I remember sitting in the car being driven to that party and wondering why I was going when I didn't know anybody there. I didn't know why I was going, my parents weren't going, I didn't want to go.

You know who I met there? Lucy Limchayseng. She got my address and I got hers. I think I had brought a little notebook.

— ∞ —

It was over at his house and they had dancing parties, and I was thirteen or fourteen. He was fifteen or sixteen. My parents were there.

I don't remember if it was at that one or another party but he invited to go swimming at Wack Wack Golf and Country Club, and we were able to go. I really wanted to go; I like swimming.

My sister went along – she was my chaperone; she was nine or ten. We liked to swim.

I remember we were just standing there and I went up to my father and asked if I could go to Wack Wack, and he said, "Next time, don't ask right in front of him," because in case he said no, that would be embarrassing, because it's right in front of him.

I remember my father saying, "If you want to ask to go out or not, don't ask it in front of the other person. You have to do it privately."

Another time he and Eddie Lim picked us up and I think we went to Wack Wack. We didn't go out many times.

— ∞ —

We counted from the time we first met each other to the time we got married how many days we actually saw each other and it was about twenty-eight days. Or less than thirty.

We first met in 1949. I was thirteen.
We went to Wack Wack.
I went to Bangkok. He went to the States.
We wrote and wrote.

In 1952 when I first came to the U.S. to go to college, he was in San Francisco on a road trip with his cousin, Manuel, who went to Berkeley. He didn't drive at the time. We saw each other for two days since he happened to be in town.

I had just arrived and was staying on Powell Street at my grandma's house. It was him, Phil, and Manuel, and we went out to eat somewhere down Washington Street. And then they brought me back home.

We saw each other for three days in New York. When I came back from Bangkok to go to Mills in '54, I ended up in New York and he took care of me. *[Pops: That was the summer I was in Wilmington.]*

In the summer of '55, he worked at a seaside resort in Connecticut, at the Dolly Madison, and I went to Connecticut. That was for about a week; that's when we got serious.

— ∞ —

I was impressed with how he got along with old people and babies equally comfortably. His landladies were old. I don't remember where the babies came from but he was able to play with babies, like when you go walking and you see babies in the park.

And he was polite. And he was very Catholic.

I wasn't Catholic at the time but he made great effort in introducing me to the faith. He sent me a lot of Catholic materials. They have a weekly newspaper at Notre Dame and he'd send it to me at Mills.

He sent me my first rosary. It's multicolored. I don't know where it is now.

When I was a freshman, he was a junior, so there were two years where we were financing the U.S. post office. Mail was three cents and postcards were one cent at that time, and we would write each other every day.

He's very polite and happy. Although at the time we got married, he was more conservative. He was more business-man-y type.

I think he was more serious, where now he might be more corny. I like to think I made him a funnier type of person. He didn't start that way, though he was a nice guy.

— ∞ —

He graduated in 1956 from Wharton and I went to the graduation in Philadelphia. I was still at Mills. I had just graduated in '56.

I remember I was asking my father if I could not go home right away to Bangkok, if I could go first to New York to attend his graduation. He didn't say anything like, "Yes you can go." He wrote something like, "We'll expect your return at such-and-such a date."

He wanted me to go to grad school and become a career woman because he thought highly of me. He thought I had potential. He wanted me to go to the American School in Lebanon. They had a well-known international school.

Sure, I would have loved to go to school in Switzerland or Lebanon, but I had a very good deal and I didn't want to give it up. I was very sure who I wanted to marry.

I kept a copy of his letter because Angkong wrote and asked for my hand in marriage, and I still have my father's letter of what he answered. At that time I was almost twenty years old, can you imagine?

It was in January and my birthday is in February, so I was actually not yet twenty.

We knew each other for eight years – 1949 to 1957 – before we got married.

— ∞ —

He never really proposed. He was so much like my father. He just said something like, "When we get to Manila, we should do this..." He never said, "Will you marry me?"

That was frustrating. He sort of assumed I was going to marry him.

He didn't ask me, so I didn't respond to anything.

So his father must have written to my father, because then my father wrote me back.

PATRICK PICHI SUN
CHINESE EMBASSY
BANGKOK

January 16, 1956

Dear Patricia:

This is a momentous letter giving you a momentous answer.

I met Larry only on few brief moments and at that time naturally I did not pay too much attention. The truth is, I don't know him well. From what you have said or suggested previously, he must be a good boy. What is good for you is good enough for me. I have your happiness at heart and I want you to be sure yourself. Now that you have considered this matter for something, I shall do everything for you in compliance to your wish. My job is to rear you up and prepare you for a happy life.

I shall ask your mother to write you separately so that you will understand her feeling.

Now you are near your graduation. This matter being decided, you shall follow your study without any let up. Do not burden yourself with too many subjects and try to make your record a fine one.

For the summer you shall come back to be with us for a few months at least. As for Sylvia, she shall be coming back soon. I thought it a good idea for her to stay up the five year period in the U.S. so that there will not be any question of her citizenship in the future. Because we have some kind of an understanding with Frances. If Frances should need her, it will unfair to pull her away any time we want her. I assure you that she is not forgotten and I for one want her to come back too.

The vital question is now after your graduation, what will you do? To get married right away? It seems a shame to turn a Phi Beta Kappa immediately into a housewife. Besides, you are still too young. In so far as I am concerned, the sooner you get married, the sooner I relieve myself of the responsibility. But just the same, I would like to see you make better use of intelligence and knowledge, for you and for humanity. I was talking to the Swiss Chargé d'Affaires about studying in Switzerland. It seems it isn't as costly as we think. There is an old Catholic University at Fribourg and one at Neuchatel. I shall collect some bulletins and catalogs and send them to you by ordinary mail. Anyway, this question will be decided after summer. Now go on with your study.

Very good luck to you and plenty of love.

Daddy

— ∞ —

Before the engagement, conventionally if you were together with someone, you got pinned. Pinning is sort of more serious than going steady. The fraternities had pins and the guys would give it to the girls. You'd be sitting at dinner and a girl would stand up and announce her pin, and everyone at the table would clap.

He gave me a pin. It was a Notre Dame pin and I wore it, and my econ professor noticed it. That was when I was a senior already. I still have it – it's either here or in Manila.

— ∞ —

My engagement ring he didn't give to me until before the wedding, because we didn't see each other until then. It was his mother's ring. It was a diamond.

The story Mama said when I got the ring was: She showed him the ring when he was a little boy, and she said, "When you get married, this is the ring that you'll give to the one who you marry."

But she says he said, "I want to marry you." He was maybe about four or five.

BECOMING CATHOLIC

I didn't know there was such a thing as the Catholic Church until I got to the Philippines. I never even heard of the Catholic Church.

I saw, when I was living on Clay Street, some girls in uniform walking by when we were standing there waiting for our carpool, and they must have been going to the Catholic school nearby, but at the time I didn't know that's what it was.

The surprise of it all was that I didn't know about the church at all until I got to Manila and that's when I was twelve years old. In Manila I had to go to Mary Knoll College for high school, and that's when I first heard of it.

It was run by American Catholic nuns. I had one year there, my sophomore year, and I transferred out later. It was during that year that I got to know about the church.

My family wasn't religious; we didn't go to church on Sundays, but we knew people who did. I think my Uncle Tim went to a Methodist church.

I got sent to Chinese school on Saturdays and it was being sponsored by an Episcopal church but it was just Chinese school, they didn't do anything church-related.

There was a Sunday school there that some neighbors wanted us to go to and I think I did go a couple of times. I remember following some book. But that was about it.

— ∞ —

So I wasn't really exposed until I went to Mills, which was a Protestant school, and I met some Catholic people. The foremost would be Angkong, because he would write to me, and he was going to Notre Dame. He would say, "This is what I've been doing," and he'd send me the newspaper, and he sent me the rosary, and he'd send me prayer cards – little stuff, just to get me interested. So he was a big help.

Then when I was a sophomore, there was a freshman who came in from Panama – Chinese. She was very religious, a little overboard, and she could hardly speak English. She spoke Spanish. She later became my godmother, and that's when we started going to mass every day.

I met a lady when we were going to mass every day and her husband became my godfather, Mr. Mollan. I wanted Angkong to be my godfather, but they said you couldn't marry your godfather.

Mrs. Mollan used to pick me up every day to go to 6 a.m. mass. She used to play the organ for the church.

mills

— ∞ —

I had special lessons. I had a special baptism because I had already been baptized in the Anglican Church.

When we were in Bangkok, we went to church. My father was more spiritual than my mother, and he thought it was the proper thing to do – for us to be attending a church. So we went to an Anglican church run by a British pastor. We got baptized as a family.

At that time I had actually wanted to become a Catholic. This was when I was about fourteen or fifteen, but I became a Protestant.

When I was at Mills I became a Catholic when I was eighteen. It was a one-on-one. The name of the church was St. Cyril's Catholic Church. I tried to look for it again online but they don't have it anymore. It's become a Korean-Mexican or something sort of church. It's not Catholic anymore. I guess they didn't have enough people.

I haven't had very much Catholic education.

— ∞ —

I was eighteen. I had my baptism on May 9th, and I had my first holy communion on May 10th, 1954. I remember my special days.

My father was very unhappy. My mother said he was very unhappy. He didn't talk to anybody for a number of days. He didn't think I should be Catholic.

The only Catholic he liked was this American priest from Baltimore who had a cigar in one hand and a cocktail in the other.

I guess the Catholics he knew were mostly old school. In those days, Catholics believed they were the only ones who were right about everybody and everyone else was pagan. I didn't think they were but I wanted very much to have my parents become Catholic.

It is so important to have a Catholic education because the foundation is important – you really have to study. It's just like Chinese or something. If you haven't been brought up with it, it's hard to make a foundation on it. It's just by example. Angkong was there.

It's good having some sort of education about the church so you know what you're doing and you learn about why people do certain things and the reasons for it. You don't get that from a class of any other kind, or church.

Some people say that if you have a Catholic education you take everything for granted, so it's better if you're a convert. So I had to fight a little bit to be a Catholic. My father didn't want me to become one but I became one anyway.

— ∞ —

Separately, when they both died, I was able to baptize them in the hospital room. It was just a private thing between them and me. Just me and a piece of cotton and some water, just in case it might have helped.

I did my mom since I was alone with her for a little bit.

The same thing happened with my father and I. We were in the room alone and I felt better about having the opportunity – I really wanted them to be baptized.

PARENTS' DEATHS

My mother had brain cancer. She was sixty-nine. When we found out, it was in September and she died in November. That was very fast.

That was, in a way, good. It's sort of sad but she went very fast. It was in San Francisco. They were living across the street from Safeway.

They were living in Manila for a while then they went to Taipei, then they were in Jamaica, then Australia, and then they retired and came to live in San Francisco in Village Square/Diamond Heights. My father wanted to retire in Taiwan but since my mom was born and brought up here, she wanted to retire here.

— ∞ —

My father was seventy-seven when he passed away. He went and stayed with my brother after my mom passed away. She died in 1981 and he passed away in 1986 – five years.

I remember Phil called on the phone. The doctor called him then he called me. Phil was so young, in his thirties.

My dad died from a series of little strokes. He had had a big stroke and was handicapped, so when he went to Houston, there was somebody we had found in Manila who was Mestiza – her father was American – and she had a U.S. Passport but she had no money to get back to the States. She came over and took care of my father.

He was in a nursing home for a while. And then he died in 1986, and now they're both buried here in the cemetery near Callan, on Hickey.

— ∞ —

That's the same one that Auntie E. is buried at, and my grandmother and grandfather – Ning Yung. Only people from a certain province in China can be buried in that cemetery so my mom said she had to die first since she's from that province.

But my grandfather, his name is Thomas Foon Chew (he was a big shot), he died at forty-two. The Chinese community which he was part of bought that cemetery. It was at a high point and it could look out at the sea.

That's where they're buried. Paula's father is there also. Janet's mother and father are there. If my father died first I don't know where he'd be buried.

BROTHER AND FATHER

Because my brother was an only son and they wanted to have one in the family so much, there was a lot of pressure on him when he was growing up.

They wanted him to be a good boy. The basic story was you wanted to protect your child and the bad spirits come to take away your child or to cause evil to your child, so you downplay them to keep them safe.

So you don't see many Chinese praising their kids saying, "Look at how good he is" or how smart he is, but instead they wouldn't make a big deal. That's true even now.

So they would put him down. And I think he internalized it. But it was done more jokingly. I don't think he really got scolded or anything like that.

But from the time I left him when he was three and I went to college, that was four years from the age of three to the age of seven, and then when I came back that was only half a year. And then I left and got married. So he didn't really have me as a sister, but Auntie Glo was there.

He was so much younger than everybody else. He was just the baby in the family, so I didn't have much chance to bond with him.

He was born in Manila. He was very, very young when we moved to Bangkok; he was three months old. There was no one to help take care of him. Mom and Dad were very busy settling down in Bangkok because at the time we arrived, the new king of Thailand was crowned and the coronation happened.

They had to go to ceremonies and parades. It was a big affair. They had elephants and stuff like that. This king – his brother had been murdered actually, and he was in Europe so he came back to get married and assume the throne when he was nineteen or twenty.

He and his wife are still respected by a lot of the Thais because he had a lot of concern for the people and developing the economy of the country. So when they had the coronation and the marriage, my father and mother had to go to all these different ceremonies and they left Philip with us when he was only three or four months, and we didn't know what to do, but my sister and I took care of him.

— ∞ —

When we left Manila on a small luxury ship, my mom wanted to give him a bath in the sink, but she wanted to sterilize it before she did. We didn't know what to use to sterilize it because there was no alcohol but someone gave her a bottle of whiskey, so they used that to sterilize it.

They made such a big deal about pouring that whiskey down the drain because when they were leaving people were sending them off on the ship and saying goodbye, and some gave a bottle of whiskey.

— ∞ —

Philip, when he was born, we were all so excited because we found out it was a boy, so Daddy said, "Let's go see a movie to celebrate." This was in Manila, and the only thing that was showing at the time was Joan of Arc.

He was born in November and we left for Bangkok in February, and he stayed in the hospital all that time with the hospital nurses in the nursery, for the first 3 months of his life. But we went to visit him every week.

We only picked him up when we were leaving to board the ship. But they had a very nice basket for him; it was a big laundry basket that was stuffed with pillows and decorated. I don't know who did it.

AUNTIE SYL

Auntie Syl. After the war we found her through the Red Cross. I remember gathering stuff to put in a box to send to her through the Red Cross. She was about five or six.

There was a couple who was taking care of her. She has a picture of them, and they wanted to adopt her but my folks made the choice.

My father was very serious. I remember him saying blood is thicker than water. They wanted her back because she was our family.

— ∞ —

She was sent to Manila because my father was transferred to Manila and that's where they met. She was at boarding school waiting for us to get there because my mom, Auntie Glo, and I weren't there yet. I had to graduate from eighth grade.

So when we came over, that was in 1948 and that was when we met her. It was so exciting having a new sister. That was when she was seven years old.

So we all went to Bangkok together in 1950. But then Auntie Fran came over with Grandma and they decided to take her back to the States because she had to establish her U.S. citizenship, because she wasn't born there and her father wasn't a U.S. citizen.

So she lived with Grandma and Auntie Fran until my father and mother went back to the States finally, around the time when Andrew was born, in 1958. And then they all lived together – she, Auntie Glo, Daddy, Mommy, and Philip.

— ∞ —

And then she got married early.

She actually ran away from home, lived on her own, and then got married. He was a nice guy.

And then she moved to Stockton.

TEACHING IN TAIPEI

After I graduated college, I joined my folks in Bangkok since that's where they were. Then we all moved to Taipei. Then I taught kindergarten at the American school in Taipei, then I quit because I got married.

School started in September and I left in January. I graduated in 1956, and got married in 1957.

— ∞ —

That was funny. Kindergarten was like twenty minute recess and it's cold in Taipei, so they'd go out and you'd button them up and by the time you finished buttoning them up and tying shoe laces, it'd be over.

There was no preparation for being a teacher. They were just so desperate to hire anyone who had U.S. degrees. Same thing for Manila.

WEDDING

In 1957, Angkong came up to Taipei for seven days with his mother before the wedding.

We planned the date and then organized what we could, me and my folks: the reception, the gown, and the place, The Grand Hotel. We got to Taipei in October and I got married in February.

We had twenty tables and we didn't really know the people. It just seemed like a lot of people. My father worked for the Taipei government as a spokesman for the Ministry of Foreign Affairs, so the tables were his staff and colleagues at the Ministry.

I had one girlfriend from Mills and her husband who attended.

— ∞ —

My brother was supposed to have the album with the pictures of the wedding, but he says he can't find it. He was there and he was seven years old, and he was very sad because I was getting married and leaving him.

The day we left he wouldn't even come to the door to say goodbye. He just sat at his table and ate his breakfast – abandonment. I was thirteen years older and we were quite close.

It was hard for him to grow up and lead a normal kiddie life because his father was an important fellow. When we were growing up, my father wasn't as important at that time so he would go to work then come home and we'd go to restaurants, and he'd help me with my homework.

— ∞ —

The wedding ceremony: It was a cold and rainy day. People said that rain means good luck.

The church was called Holy Family Church, small. I think that was the church we were going to. It was nearby. It was really hard to get inside from car to church without getting wet. The roof was leaking down the aisle, so what preceded me down the aisle was a janitor with a mop.

My sister was not bridesmaid or maid of honor because she lost her front tooth and didn't have a replacement yet or something like that, so she opted out. I had no flower girls.

[Pops: I had the ring in my pocket. I was the ring bearer.]

His mom came, and there was a sponsor – a businessman who represented us as our ninong for the wedding. He was a businessman friend of my father-in-law's, Fernando Remedios.

We had a mass. I think there was no choir. The small church was pretty full.

All I can remember was it was very cold. My mom got sick afterwards because she didn't wear a jacket because the dress was nice. She caught the flu or something.

— ∞ —

The priest that married us was Father Albert O'Hara, SJ, who Angkong and his father and mother knew in Manila because that priest worked in Manila before.

At the banquet, we forgot to ask someone to pick up the priest from his residence.

— ∞ —

Taiwan was under martial law at the time. They had just come away from mainland China.

So how did this affect my wedding gown? You could not purchase a wedding gown. You go to the store and you could only rent a gown, and you had to return it in three days because it passes on to someone else. They had to conserve luxury items, and this was a luxury item.

If you didn't like the availability of what they offered to rent, you could design one, but you'd have to return it.

So the wedding gown cost twelve U.S. dollars to rent. If I had chosen one off the rack it would have been even cheaper.

We made it a little fancier; we added pearl eyelets, little pearls sewn in, and you could have it out of nicer material. I think my mom probably asked what was the best available then tried to get better. I don't think it had a train.

My mom had a friend and she helped us out with this since she spoke Mandarin.

That's how they did it in those days since they only had so much nice materials, and then we just returned everything.

— ∞ —

Because of martial law and the lack of luxury items, if people wanted to give you gifts there wasn't anything to buy. All they had was plenty of roses. I got lots and lots of roses.

There weren't any household goods. What they had was things made out of silver, like the little Clipper ship sitting on the tables in the living room at Galaxy; nothing of household value, but lots and lots of flowers, and maybe little statues. No rice cookers or anything like that.

[Pops: The whole church was filled with red roses.] That's all they had in those days.

Taipei in those days, everyone got rations. They got some rice, oil, and some salt. It was like social security.

When we were in Taipei, we had a husband and wife helper; he was a pedicab driver and she was a cook and a housemaid. That's how I got to school when I was teaching at Taipei American School before I got married.

— ∞ —

We stayed at The Grand Hotel the night of the banquet. Then we took a train to Sun Moon Lake for our honeymoon, a famous resort in Taiwan. We ended up going home early.

[Pops: The first night we were there, soldiers came knocking on the door. They thought we were doing something illegal. We had to prove we were married.] And we didn't know enough Chinese to really have a conversation. We did a tour of Sun Moon Lake, we went a little bit around the lake and saw some aboriginal dancing – it was somewhat of a tourist thing – and then we went back.

[Pops: After the honeymoon we went back to Taipei for a few days then to Manila to start our new life.]

We went to Manila on my birthday actually. Actually the first time we went to Manila was on my birthday. Then things happened and years passed, and then the next time we went back to Manila was also my birthday.

— ∞ —

My wedding ring, he chose it in Manila. It had seven diamonds in it, representing nothing really. If we had seven kids it would've been that, but we had six – Andrew, Melanie, Tom, Geeg, Ken, and Mike.

One diamond fell out and never got replaced when he had his aneurism operation here at St. Mary's in 2005, and I sort of figured, well, it's easy giving up a diamond for a life. That was the basic idea.

FIRST PREGNANCY

He started work a week after at Philippine American Life Insurance Company (Phil-Am Life). His new position was as a staff assistant at 600 pesos; a staff assistant to the agent manager in charge of all the agents.

I started teaching at American School in June in Pasay City in Manila. I worked for three months and then I had an operation because I had pain.

I was pregnant and developed a twisted ovary. They removed the ovary and I was in the hospital for about a week.

The doctor who operated was very famous, Dr. Pacifico Yap. He was ambidextrous and he won sharp shooting championships and operated on presidents. His son was a doctor at Seton here. This was in 1957.

My OBGYN knew I was pregnant two months and gave me some steroids so I wouldn't have a miscarriage. We found out later on that it may have been too much because the baby was supposed to be born in January but was born in March. He was a post-mature baby.

I went to the hospital for a cesarean but delivered normally the night before.

— ∞ —

When I was in the hospital for the first operation, everyone thought I was for sure going to lose the baby, and I lost an ovary and that was an important part of the reproductive system.

And then the other myth they had was that with only one ovary you'd have all boys or all girls.

Or the other was that I would not be able to have kids at all. My sister-in-law was pregnant with her second child and she offered that we could adopt her baby.

CHILDREN & TEACHING IN MANILA

When we got to Manila, I taught at the American school there – third grade and fifth grade, and summer school second grade.

And then I stopped because the kids were born every year so I tutored instead, at home.

With the American school and the population there, people would come in at all times of the year and have to catch up. They would take the tests and find out they're lagging in whatever and they'd be referred to me, and I would teach them whatever they missed out on.

It was good because they would come to the house, and if they didn't come, I was still at home. I did that for years. And I was doing it sometimes up to eight hours a day.

That was all at Galaxy. I had mostly all of the kids. We had maids taking care of the kids, but the older ones would go to school.

The nice thing about having so many kids was that they all played with each other and they never got into big fights. It was like if somebody wasn't pleasant, you would go play with someone else who was pleasant.

It was really only Mei and Tom who got into each other's hair. Andrew was quiet and friendly with everyone.

— ∞ —

Meanwhile my folks were in Taipei. Then they went to San Francisco, then he was assigned to Manila around 1968 or '69, to 1972 or '73.

— ∞ —

You needed to have both your father and mother to pass on U.S. citizenship, and you had to reside in the U.S. yourself ten years after the age of fourteen, so I couldn't pass on citizenship to the kids directly. They had to go to the American embassy and apply for immigration status.

They had a special category but they had to go through all the procedures. We had to do it every year and it was such a pain, but other people had to wait years and years and they didn't have to wait.

When they went to the States it was all Filipino citizenship, but it was a special priority visa.

I couldn't pass it on because I didn't live in the States long enough after the age of fourteen.

— ∞ —

When Uncle Andrew and Auntie Mei and everybody started going to college, they'd have to go through Hawaii, so they'd stay with my friend Vivian. Viv would go pick them up from the airport then bring them back.

Kenneth was her husband. They lived with her mother-in-law for the longest time. They had a daughter first, Cheryl, and a son, Sherwin, and he talked so much. When we were there he was three years old, and he kept on talking and talking. I've never seen someone talk so much. He grew up to be a lawyer.

They live in Honolulu on a street called Fern Street.

Q & A TODAY

What is one thing you have always wanted but still don't have?

I won't get it anymore. To get another degree – a Master's in Sociology. At Ateneo I did all the requirements except the dissertation. I spent two years doing night classes. I drove up there and drove back.

When the kids were all born I didn't have a chance; there wasn't spare time. When they all went to high school and some went to college 1976-78, I did it for two years. I was so close. Every time I tried to finish they added a new requirement.

My parents came to Manila to stay so I spent time with them instead.

You take a master test on all the subjects you've ever taken, the Comprehensive, your two years of classes. So I passed that already, but then came the dissertation and I stopped there.

The work that you do for that – when you've gotten that degree, you know all this theoretical stuff, but there's more than that to the field. It was so academic. When I was growing up I was always geared towards the academic but that's as far as I got.

— ∞ —

How are you like or unlike your parents?

I'm more confident in meeting people. I'm an introvert, but my parents were more outgoing and I guess I'm more like them. When I was a teenager I sure wasn't.

My father was very methodical. He followed rules. If you were supposed to be at a certain place at a certain time, he was strict about that.

My mom was very friendly with everybody, that's what I really liked about her. Maybe I take after her in that way. My mom when she came over to Manila, she came and was chit chatting with the maids. Tai Ma would never do that since it was a status thing.

His mom was brought up in Hong Kong. There's a lot of social structure there, whereas my mom was from here.

— ∞ —

What is the best compliment you ever received?

I had to introduce the president of our college at a meeting in Manila and someone said they thought I was a member of the Toastmasters Club.

— ∞ —

What is the highest honor or award you have ever received?

Angkong says marriage proposal. Larry, you're just so full of it. *[Pops: Call me Donald.]*

When I was a junior in college, I was accepted into an honor society called Phi Beta Kappa. It was an honor to be a junior accepted into it. It's hard to get in in the first place and being a junior was special.

— ∞ —

What kinds of things do you enjoy now and when you were a child?

Good rest and sleep at night. Because I don't sleep so well at night, in the daytime I'm tired. Reading magazines about world events.

I liked tennis when the kids were younger. We played at the Polo Club maybe once or twice. I played with friends while the kids were in school. And swimming.

Skating. Roller skating. I did a good job on roller skates on the hills of San Francisco.

— ∞ —

What things frighten you now and when you were a child?

Used to be spiders. I'm not as scared of them anymore. Well I wouldn't want to meet up with one, but it's not as bad as it used to be.

Firecrackers. The noise scares me. Same thing before.

Now, a little claustrophobic with scuba diving gear. We did that in the Philippines, maybe about fifteen or twenty years ago. I was surprised at myself because I like swimming, and then all of a sudden I got claustrophobic.

People usually get trained to scuba dive in a swimming pool. I didn't get a chance to do that; this was just someone's resort with Mike and Tin. I went down a little bit and then came back and wanted it off. I would've thought it would be really wonderful to go down.

But I didn't have nightmares about it.

— ∞ —

If you could have three wishes, what would they be?

One for family: Health and happiness and ability to prioritize correctly according to their values, like the general rules about caring and sharing with others. I think I've tried to show what's important to us, setting a good example. That's been one of my priorities, in a quiet way.

One for everybody else in the world: I'd like to wish for more peace and understanding in world situations, where everybody could not be so selfishly thinking of their own gain. We watched TV last night, the 60 Minutes section about mindfulness. That may help towards it. It really helps, so you don't get so frazzled about the future and the past. Maybe there are solutions to present day problems because they're not mindful enough. There's something more to life than what their brains are spitting out – people opening up to listen to the other side. You know sometimes people go into a session with fixed ideas already and don't give the other side a chance to be heard.

One for Angkong: Long happy life. Well it was my little pet project, you know. It's good he's working a little harder these days, more exercise.

— ∞ —

If you won a million dollars tomorrow, what would you do with the money?

Work on projects that Angkong likes. That would do it. Use it to fund scholarships, down payments…

— ∞ —

Do you feel differently about yourself now from how you felt when you were younger?

I guess everybody would. I'm more confident in my decisions. I feel I have more perspective in situations; more tolerant of disagreements.

And then this thing about where you fit in the pattern of life, sort of the meaning of your existence – I'm more confident of that. It fluctuates you know, sometimes you feel more confident and sometimes you feel, Is this all there is to me?

I had a project and I feel it was successful.

— ∞ —

What do you think has stayed the same about you throughout life?

I think emotionally, I'm still a very quiet type of person. Quiet and steady. I don't make big waves.

Happy 80th Birthday, Ah Ma!

— ∞ —

February 22, 2016

www.ingramcontent.com/pod-product-compliance
Ingram Content Group UK Ltd.
Pitfield, Milton Keynes, MK11 3LW, UK
UKHW040559210726
13854UKWH00008B/1553